Published in 2015 by The Rosen Publishing Group, Inc.
29 East 21st Street, New York, NY 10010

Photo Credits: **KEY** tl=top left; bl=bottom left; br=bottom right

CBT = Corbis; iS = istockphoto.com; SH = Shutterstock; TPL = photolibrary.com

Cover SH; **7**bl SH; **9**br TPL; **13**br SH; **24**tl iS; **25**tl CBT

All illustrations copyright Weldon Owen Pty Ltd

WELDON OWEN PTY LTD
Managing Director: Kay Scarlett
Creative Director: Sue Burk
Publisher: Helen Bateman
Senior Vice President, International Sales: Stuart Laurence
Vice President Sales North America: Ellen Towell
Administration Manager, International Sales: Kristine Ravn

Library of Congress Cataloging-in-Publication Data

Stephens, David, 1945–
  Sharks : predators of the ocean / by David Stephens.
     pages cm. — (Discovery education. Animals)
  Includes index.
  ISBN 978-1-4777-6926-3 (library binding) — ISBN 978-1-4777-6927-0 (pbk.) —
ISBN 978-1-4777-6928-7 (6-pack)
  1. Sharks—Juvenile literature. I. Title.
  QL638.9.S8446 2015
  597.3—dc23
                         2013047593

Manufactured in the United States of America

CPSIA Compliance Information: Batch #WS14PK3: For Further Information contact Rosen Publishing, New York, New York at 1-800-237-9932

ANIMALS

SHARKS
PREDATORS OF THE OCEAN

David Stephens

PowerKiDS
press
New York

Contents

Fish With Attitude 6

Evolution 8

Types of Sharks.....................................10

Inside the Perfect Predator.................12

Nowhere to Hide 14

Bite Time 16

Shark Diet..18

Built for Speed.....................................20

Habitats 22

Up Close and Personal 24

You Decide 26

Endangered...28

Mix and Match 30

Glossary..31

Index 32

Websites...32

Fish With Attitude

Zebra shark

Sharks are a type of fish. Unlike other fish, sharks live for 40 years or more and are born ready to hunt for food. Sharks have a light skeleton that is made of soft cartilage instead of bone. Their skin is rough like sandpaper, not scaly and slippery like other fish.

Chain catshark

Caudal fin

First dorsal fin

Second dorsal fin

Anal fin

Pelvic fin

Oceanic whitetip

Whale shark

This gentle giant is the world's largest living fish and will often allow divers to swim alongside it.

Shark tails

The tail, or caudal fin, pushes the shark through the water. Fast swimmers have a large, curved tail. Slow swimmers have a smaller, flat tail.

Thresher shark

That's Amazing!

Fishermen have reported spotting huge whale sharks that are one and a half times the length of a regular school bus.

Horn shark

Blacktip reef shark

Great white shark

Shark fins

These are necessary for a shark's buoyancy and lift. They also help sharks to accelerate, brake, and turn while swimming.

Sharks come in all sizes, ranging from the 7 inch (18 cm) spined pygmy shark to the 40 foot (12 m) whale shark.

Gill slits

Eye

Frilled shark

Mouth

Spined pygmy shark

Pectoral fin

False catshark

Shark snouts

The shape of these tells us how a shark feeds, such as digging in the ocean floor, snapping at passing fish, or cracking open shellfish.

Filter feeder

The whale shark sucks water into its mouth, then filters it out through its gills, capturing tiny marine creatures to eat.

Black dogfish shark

Evolution

About 240 million years before dinosaurs were roaming Earth, odd-looking shark ancestors hunted the oceans. Some of these sharks had curly teeth, while others had strange bristles on their head.

Evolution time line

How sharks evolved during ancient periods

* mya = million years ago

280 mya *Helicoprion*
This shark had a spiral set of teeth at the end of its lower jaw.

505 mya
During the Ordovician period, sharks evolved from this Thelodont.

408 mya
In the Devonian period, fish diversified. The *Ctenacanthus* had spines in front of its dorsal fins.

550 mya
In the Cambrian period, animals with shells and jawless fish evolved. Trilobites looked like giant bugs.

435 mya
The first bony fish, such as this *Nostolepsis*, appeared during the Silurian period.

360 mya
The scissor-toothed shark evolved during the Carboniferous period.

370 mya *Cladoselache*
This shark was unusual among ancient sharks because of its long keel fins.

320 mya *Stethacanthus*
The male had a "scrub brush" on its head and first dorsal fin, which was possibly used during mating.

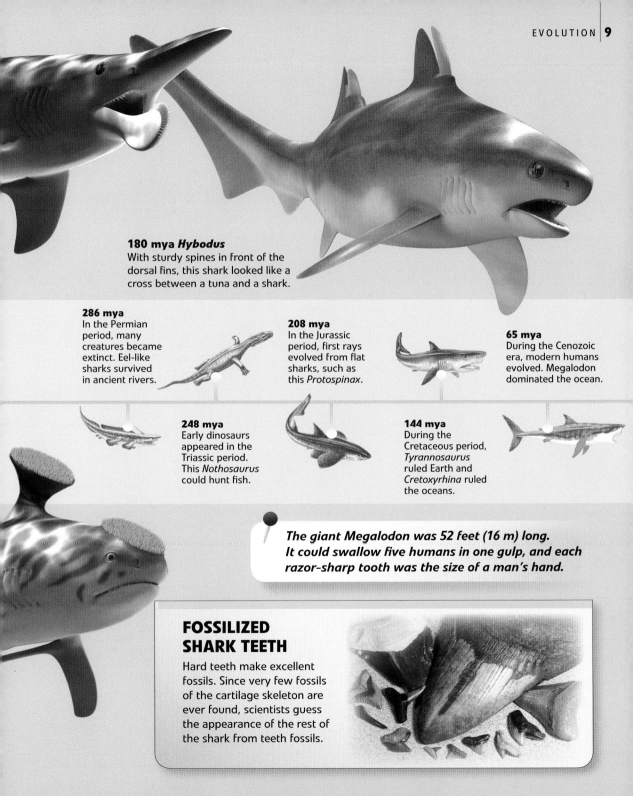

180 mya *Hybodus*
With sturdy spines in front of the dorsal fins, this shark looked like a cross between a tuna and a shark.

286 mya
In the Permian period, many creatures became extinct. Eel-like sharks survived in ancient rivers.

208 mya
In the Jurassic period, first rays evolved from flat sharks, such as this *Protospinax*.

65 mya
During the Cenozoic era, modern humans evolved. Megalodon dominated the ocean.

248 mya
Early dinosaurs appeared in the Triassic period. This *Nothosaurus* could hunt fish.

144 mya
During the Cretaceous period, *Tyrannosaurus* ruled Earth and *Cretoxyrhina* ruled the oceans.

The giant Megalodon was 52 feet (16 m) long. It could swallow five humans in one gulp, and each razor-sharp tooth was the size of a man's hand.

FOSSILIZED SHARK TEETH

Hard teeth make excellent fossils. Since very few fossils of the cartilage skeleton are ever found, scientists guess the appearance of the rest of the shark from teeth fossils.

Types of Sharks

There are more than 400 species of sharks in the oceans. Scientists have divided them into eight groups, or orders. These orders are based on classifications relating to shark features, such as the number of gills and the shape of teeth.

PORT JACKSON SHARK

ORDER: Heterodontiformes

SIZE: 5.5 feet (1.7 m)

DIET: Sea urchins, starfish, barnacles, and sea snails

HABITAT: Southern Australian oceans, from tidal to continental depths

ANGEL SHARK

ORDER: Squatiniformes

SIZE: 6.5 feet (2 m)

DIET: Small fish, crustaceans, squid, and mollusks

HABITAT: Bottom dwellers in warm oceans

BROADNOSE SHARK

ORDER: Hexanchiformes

SIZE: 10 feet (3 m)

DIET: Larger animals such as sharks, rays, seals, and seabirds

HABITAT: Temperate to tropical seas at continental shelf edges

BRAMBLE SHARK

ORDER: Squaliformes

SIZE: Up to 10 feet (3 m)

DIET: A variety of bottom prey

HABITAT: Found at depths around 3,000 feet (900 m)

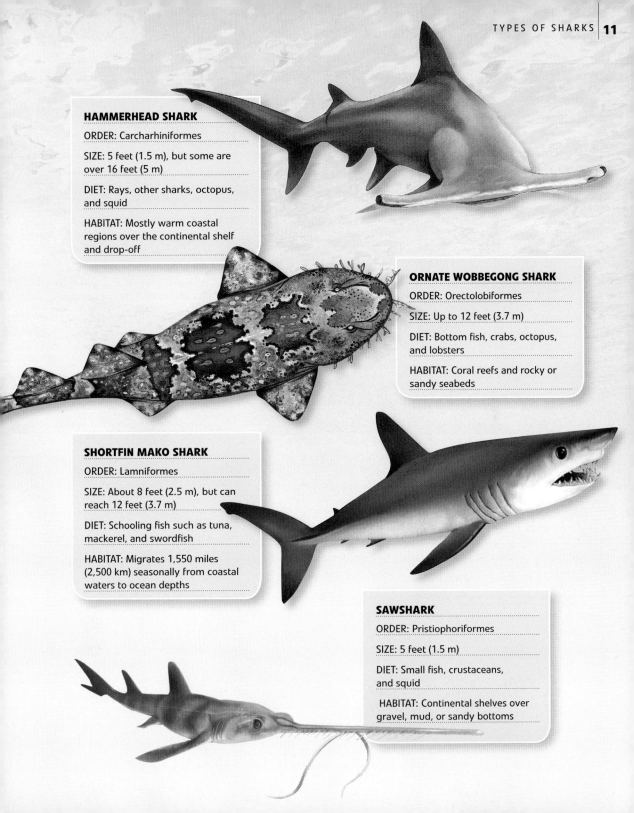

HAMMERHEAD SHARK

ORDER: Carcharhiniformes

SIZE: 5 feet (1.5 m), but some are over 16 feet (5 m)

DIET: Rays, other sharks, octopus, and squid

HABITAT: Mostly warm coastal regions over the continental shelf and drop-off

ORNATE WOBBEGONG SHARK

ORDER: Orectolobiformes

SIZE: Up to 12 feet (3.7 m)

DIET: Bottom fish, crabs, octopus, and lobsters

HABITAT: Coral reefs and rocky or sandy seabeds

SHORTFIN MAKO SHARK

ORDER: Lamniformes

SIZE: About 8 feet (2.5 m), but can reach 12 feet (3.7 m)

DIET: Schooling fish such as tuna, mackerel, and swordfish

HABITAT: Migrates 1,550 miles (2,500 km) seasonally from coastal waters to ocean depths

SAWSHARK

ORDER: Pristiophoriformes

SIZE: 5 feet (1.5 m)

DIET: Small fish, crustaceans, and squid

HABITAT: Continental shelves over gravel, mud, or sandy bottoms

Inside the Perfect Predator

As well as a heart, brain, stomach, and kidneys similar to humans, sharks also have gills for breathing underwater and a liver filled with oil that helps to keep them afloat. Extra blood vessels in its swimming muscles, brain, and eyes keep sharks alert and ready for action.

Inside a salmon shark

Salmon sharks live in the cold North Pacific Ocean, where they eat their favorite food, salmon. They have extra networks of blood vessels to keep their blood warm.

Reproductive organs

Intestines

CARTILAGE SKELETON

A shark's skeleton is made of soft cartilage similar to human ears. Cartilage is lighter than bone, and makes it easier for a shark to swim.

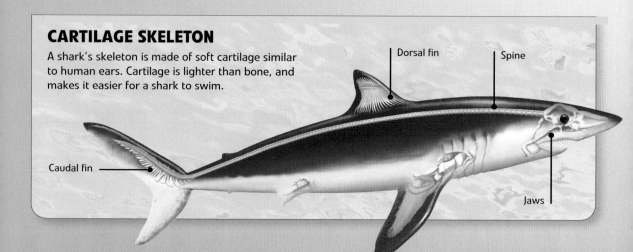

Dorsal fin

Spine

Caudal fin

Jaws

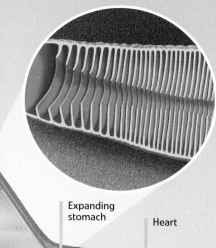

Spiral valve
Sharks have short intestines, so the inside is made like a spiral to provide a large surface area for digesting food.

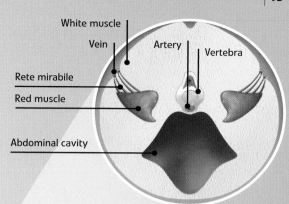

White muscle

Vein

Artery

Vertebra

Rete mirabile

Red muscle

Abdominal cavity

Expanding stomach

Heart

Gill slits

Brain

Rete mirabile
This cross-section shows two of the four networks of fine blood vessels that warm cold blood coming from the gills. A salmon shark can keep its blood temperature at a comfortable 78°F (26°C), despite ice-cold waters.

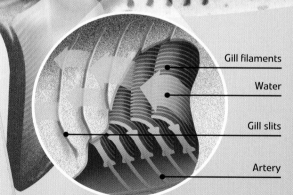

Gill filaments

Water

Gill slits

Artery

Liver

How gills work
Water enters the shark's mouth and flows out across the gill filaments. Blood in the gills flows in the opposite direction, picking up oxygen from the water.

Gills up close
Sharks have five to seven gill slits, and sometimes an extra one called a spiracle. The spiracle allows a shark to breathe with a mouth filled with food. Most sharks need to keep moving to breathe.

Nowhere to Hide

Sharks have an awesome array of senses. They hear and feel a thrashing fish 1,650 feet (500 m) away, and their directional sense of smell detects blood in the water up to 80 feet (25 m) away. Their excellent eyesight allows them to see in low light and up close. Electrical sensors in their snout guide their final, fatal bite.

A shark's sensory trail

Here is how a shark uses its senses to hunt a bluefin tuna.

HAMMERHEAD VISION

Hammerhead sharks have eyes on either side of their wing-shaped head. This gives great side vision, but they must swing their head from side to side to see forward.

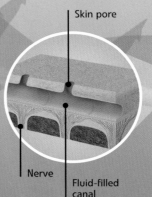

Skin pore

Nerve

Fluid-filled canal

1 Hearing

Tiny holes on the head connect to the inner ear, which detects sound waves in the water. Semicircular canals in the ear maintain balance.

2 Smell

Inside the shark's nostrils, water containing the tuna scent flows across a group of sensing membranes called lamellae.

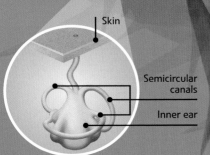

Skin

Semicircular canals

Inner ear

5 Electroreceptors

The ampullae of Lorenzini are jelly-filled pits on the shark's snout. They contain sensors that detect minute electrical currents caused when muscles contract. This shark can sense the tuna's heart beating.

4 Pressure detection

Under the skin is the lateral line—a system of fluid-filled canals that act like motion sensors. They detect the smallest pressure changes in the water.

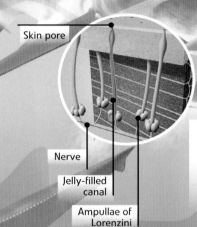

Skin pore

Nerve

Jelly-filled canal

Ampullae of Lorenzini

6 Taste

Shark taste buds are in its mouth and gullet, not on the tongue like human taste buds.

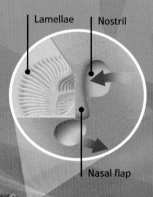

Lamellae   Nostril

Nasal flap

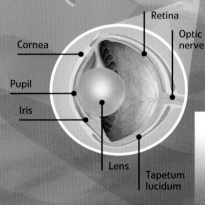

Cornea

Pupil

Iris

Lens

Retina

Optic nerve

Tapetum lucidum

3 Vision

Shark eyes have a special lining called tapetum lucidum to improve vision at dawn and dusk, when the shark hunts.

When hunting, the fastest swimming shark is the shortfin mako. It reaches speeds of 31 miles (50 km) per hour.

Bite Time

No escape
A shark's cartilage jaws are hinged just behind the head and held in place with powerful muscles.

Jaw relaxes
As it prepares to bite, a shark's jaw relaxes and its mouth starts to open.

Jaw moves forward
As the lower jaw drops, the snout tilts up and the upper jaw pushes forward.

Teeth appear
As the mouth opens wider, the eyes roll back to protect them from the prey, and the teeth stand up ready to pierce the skin of this little sandbar shark.

When a shark attacks, it moves its jaw forward to allow teeth to do maximum damage to its prey. A tiger shark can bite down with a force of 3 tons per square inch (422 kg/cm^2). If a shark breaks or loses teeth, another row grows into place.

Great teeth for a great white shark

This shark is the owner of the world's largest shark teeth. When it grabs its prey, it shakes its head from side to side so the razor-sharp teeth act like mini saws.

A TOOTH FOR EVERY MEAL

Sharks' teeth are tailored to suit the prey they feed on.

Tiger shark
Sawing and smashing teeth of the tiger shark can tackle a turtle shell.

Pale goblin shark
Spearing teeth of the pale goblin shark can pin down wriggling squid.

Kitefin shark
Serrated lower and hooked upper teeth of the kitefin shark are ideal for grabbing whole fish.

Great white shark
Sawlike teeth of the great white shark slice up seals and other large prey.

Filter feeders
Only three species of shark are filter feeders—the basking, the whale, and the megamouth. The megamouth has light-producing organs around its mouth to attract plankton, and the basking shark swims with its mouth open.

Basking shark

Megamouth shark

Shark Diet

Sharks usually eat meat, although some sharks will eat just about anything. Scientists who examined the contents of tiger shark stomachs after they were caught found everything from shoes to buckets and, one time, even a suit of armor.

Blue shark banquet
When millions of market squid swarm together to find mates, blue sharks will swim through the middle and gulp down huge mouthfuls.

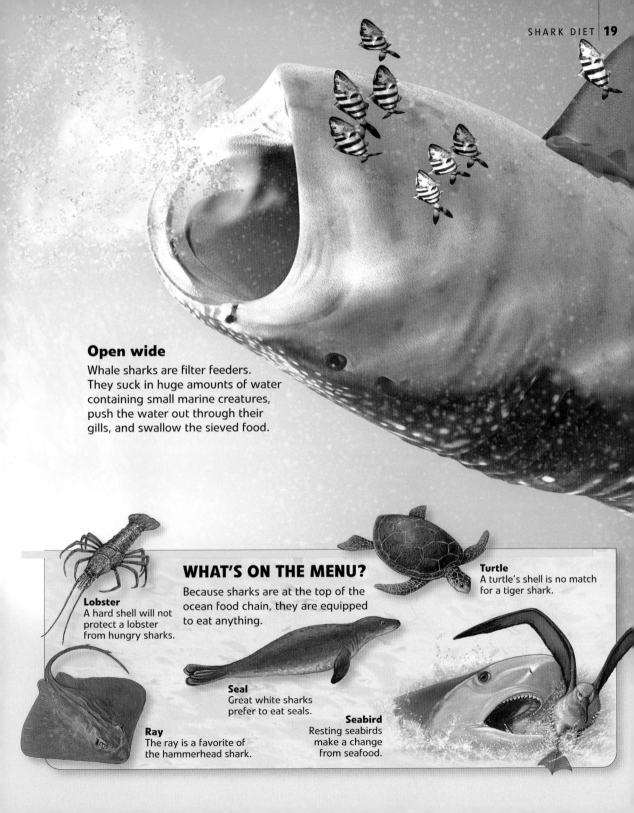

Open wide

Whale sharks are filter feeders.
They suck in huge amounts of water
containing small marine creatures,
push the water out through their
gills, and swallow the sieved food.

WHAT'S ON THE MENU?

Because sharks are at the top of the
ocean food chain, they are equipped
to eat anything.

Lobster
A hard shell will not
protect a lobster
from hungry sharks.

Turtle
A turtle's shell is no match
for a tiger shark.

Seal
Great white sharks
prefer to eat seals.

Seabird
Resting seabirds
make a change
from seafood.

Ray
The ray is a favorite of
the hammerhead shark.

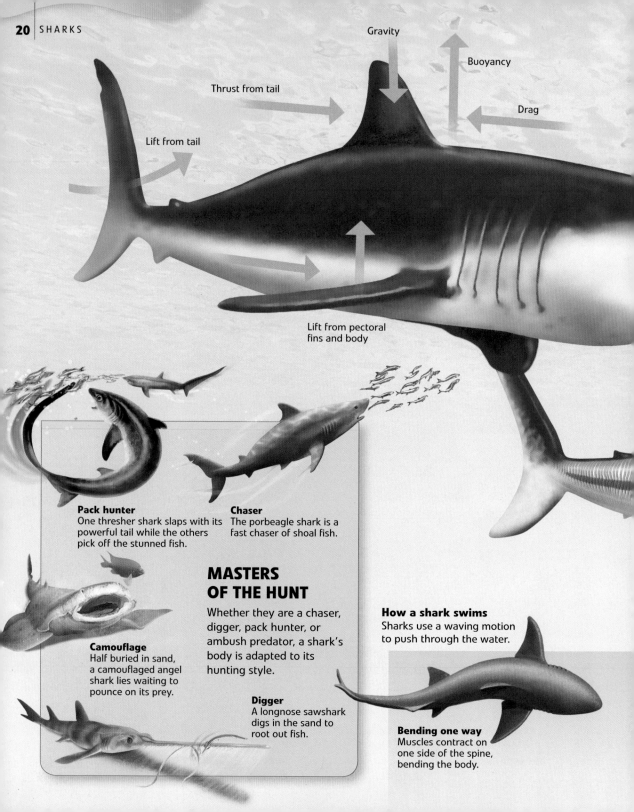

Gravity

Buoyancy

Thrust from tail

Drag

Lift from tail

Lift from pectoral
fins and body

Pack hunter
One thresher shark slaps with its
powerful tail while the others
pick off the stunned fish.

Chaser
The porbeagle shark is a
fast chaser of shoal fish.

MASTERS
OF THE HUNT

Whether they are a chaser,
digger, pack hunter, or
ambush predator, a shark's
body is adapted to its
hunting style.

How a shark swims
Sharks use a waving motion
to push through the water.

Camouflage
Half buried in sand,
a camouflaged angel
shark lies waiting to
pounce on its prey.

Digger
A longnose sawshark
digs in the sand to
root out fish.

Bending one way
Muscles contract on
one side of the spine,
bending the body.

Built for Speed

Shaped like a torpedo
The shortfin mako has the body and crescent tail of a high-speed underwater athlete.

Most sharks must keep swimming to force water over their gills. If they stop, they will suffocate. Buoyancy and lift provided by its liver, pectoral fin, and tail help the shark resist the pull of gravity and prevent it from sinking. Thrust from the tail drives the shark forward against the drag of the water. Even the tough, scaly skin is designed to reduce friction.

Mako sharks have the muscle power to leap from the water like a missile. They have frightened many fishermen by actually landing in their boat.

Red muscle

White muscle

Muscle power
About 65 percent of this shark's body weight is swimming muscle. The red muscle is used to cruise along, while the zigzag lines of white muscle are used for speed.

Thrusting forward
The body straightens and the tail thrusts the shark forward.

Bending the other way
Muscles on the other side of the spine contract and the body bends the other way.

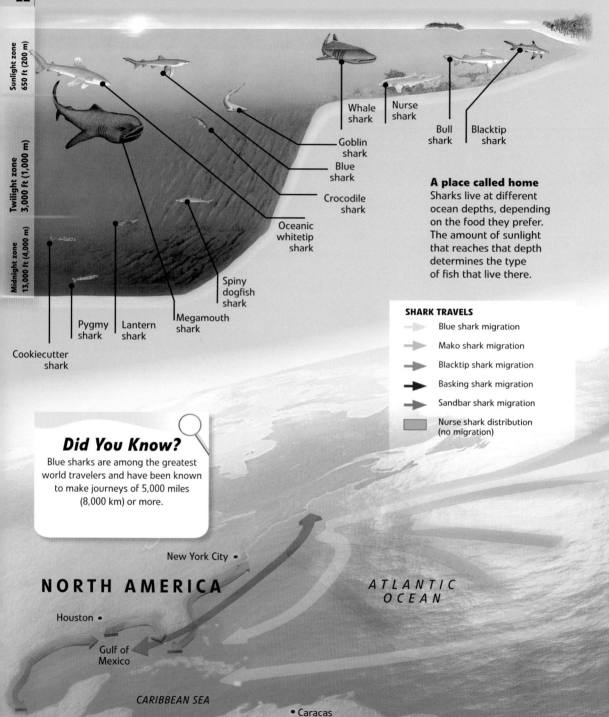

Sunlight zone
650 ft (200 m)

Twilight zone
3,000 ft (1,000 m)

Midnight zone
13,000 ft (4,000 m)

Whale
shark

Nurse
shark

Bull
shark

Blacktip
shark

Goblin
shark

Blue
shark

Crocodile
shark

Oceanic
whitetip
shark

Spiny
dogfish
shark

Megamouth
shark

Pygmy
shark

Lantern
shark

Cookiecutter
shark

A place called home
Sharks live at different
ocean depths, depending
on the food they prefer.
The amount of sunlight
that reaches that depth
determines the type
of fish that live there.

SHARK TRAVELS

Blue shark migration

Mako shark migration

Blacktip shark migration

Basking shark migration

Sandbar shark migration

Nurse shark distribution
(no migration)

Did You Know?
Blue sharks are among the greatest
world travelers and have been known
to make journeys of 5,000 miles
(8,000 km) or more.

New York City ●

NORTH AMERICA

*ATLANTIC
OCEAN*

Houston ●

Gulf of
Mexico

CARIBBEAN SEA

● Caracas

SOUTH AMERICA

Habitats

Sharks can be found in almost any marine environment. Some prefer swimming in deep waters, while others enjoy shallow, coastal areas. Some travel thousands of miles (km) to find a mate or to follow migrating fish. Others look for water that is just the right temperature.

HOME FOR SHARK PUPS

Mangrove forests that grow on the edge of oceans are the birthplace of many water creatures, including sharks. Conservationists are trying to stop these important breeding grounds from disappearing as a result of coastal development.

ASIA

ATLANTIC
OCEAN

London

Paris

EUROPE

MEDITERRANEAN
SEA

Madrid

Rabat

AFRICA

Migration mysteries

Until recently, scientists had no idea how far sharks traveled. Today, sharks are tagged with tiny satellite positioning devices, and studies show that they make journeys of thousands of miles (km) around the globe.

Dakar

Up Close and Personal

Much of what is known about sharks has come from studying dead ones. Scientists today, however, are more interested in observing live ones. This requires a great deal of patience because it is impossible to swim with sharks 24 hours a day. Sharks are tagged and tracked. This is a risky business but there are many ways to protect the observer.

Photographing sharks
Waving your arms at a shark is like an invitation to lunch. Undersea photographers keep their bodies very still so the sharks do not feel threatened.

Did You Know?
Many sharks go into a trancelike state and become immobile when flipped onto their back. Once righted, they swim off as if nothing happened.

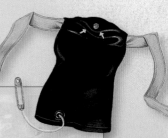

KEEPING SHARKS AT BAY
There are a few safety devices to chase off nosey sharks should you happen to be in the water with one.

US Navy shark bag
This bag is designed for surviving at sea.

Shark-proof vest
Specially designed life vests have a chemical repellent.

Protective Oceanic Device
Attached to flippers or a surfboard, protective oceanic devices (PODs) produce a strong electric field that repels sharks.

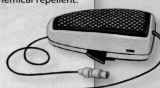

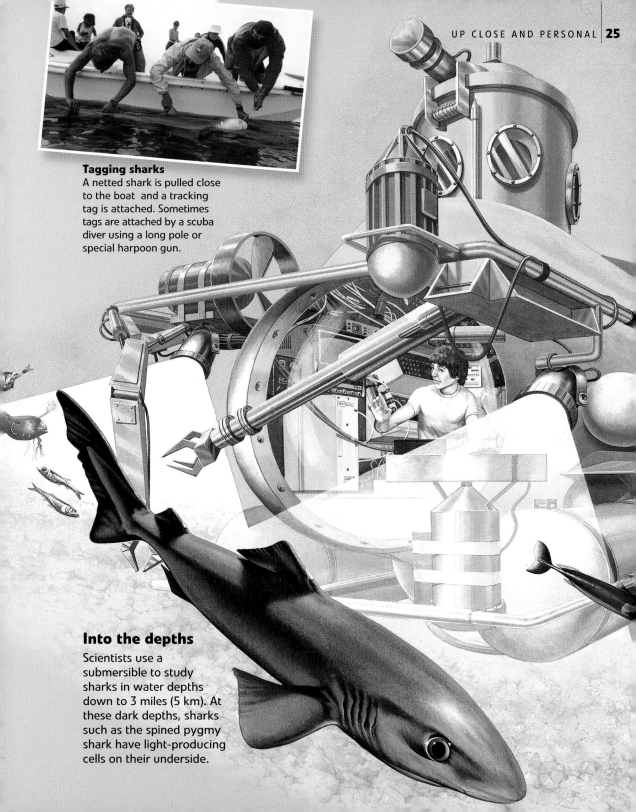

Tagging sharks

A netted shark is pulled close to the boat and a tracking tag is attached. Sometimes tags are attached by a scuba diver using a long pole or special harpoon gun.

Into the depths

Scientists use a submersible to study sharks in water depths down to 3 miles (5 km). At these dark depths, sharks such as the spined pygmy shark have light-producing cells on their underside.

?... You Decide

More than 100 million sharks die in fishing nets every year, and their breeding grounds are being destroyed by human activity and pollution. Many sharks need to reach the age of between 10 and 20 years before they can breed, so it is no wonder they are under threat. On the other hand, are they a threat to humans?

Trapped by nets
Sharks, rays, and even dolphins often become tangled in fishing nets. Unable to swim, a shark will drown through lack of oxygen.

WHAT ARE THE ODDS?

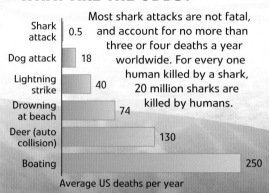

Most shark attacks are not fatal, and account for no more than three or four deaths a year worldwide. For every one human killed by a shark, 20 million sharks are killed by humans.

Shark attack	0.5
Dog attack	18
Lightning strike	40
Drowning at beach	74
Deer (auto collision)	130
Boating	250

Average US deaths per year

More curious than aggressive

Most sharks use their mouth to "feel" things they do not understand. Experts believe that only the bull, great white, mako, and tiger sharks are threatening to humans.

PRODUCTS TO DIE FOR

Sharks have been killed for use in medicine, food, cosmetics, and other products.

Food
Shark meat is eaten, but often only the dorsal fin is cut off to make an expensive Asian soup.

Medicine
The clear covering that protects a shark's eye is used to repair damaged human eyes.

Cosmetics
Shark oil is used in some lipsticks, creams, and lotions.

Dietary supplements
Sharks' liver oil contains vitamin A and is used in vitamin pills.

Endangered

More than 60 species of shark are under threat of possible extinction. Overfishing and being caught in nets and long drag lines are causing a steep drop in shark numbers. Sharks are the oceans' top predators. Without them, the balance of life in the oceans will be seriously affected.

BASKING SHARK

This harmless shark has a slow reproduction rate, and has been overfished for its huge liver.

STRIPED SMOOTH-HOUND SHARK

This small shark is easily caught in fishing nets and has almost disappeared from its home waters off South America.

SAND TIGER SHARK

This shark has only two pups every two years, so even killing just a few adults affects their numbers.

ANGEL SHARK

Trawler nets that scrape along the ocean floor capture many angel sharks. They are mostly thrown back but usually do not survive.

DAGGERNOSE SHARK

This shark has been overfished in its home waters, off the coast of Venezuela, and has now almost disappeared.

GULPER SHARK

This shark prefers deep waters. It gives birth only every two years. It is fished heavily around its native area, Taiwan.

GREAT WHITE SHARK

This shark has only one pup every two to three years and does not breed until it is 10 years old. In the past 50 years, the drop in their numbers is estimated at between 60 and 95 percent, making the species very vulnerable.

Mix and Match

In this book, you will find many interesting facts about different sharks. On this page, they have all been mixed up. You have to match the shark on the left with an interesting fact about them on the right. The answers are at the bottom of the page.

A

B

A	B
Whale shark	wing-shaped head
Megalodon	fast chaser of shoal fish
Pygmy shark	migrates the greatest distance
Shortfin mako shark	largest teeth
Great white shark	lives near Venezuela
Porbeagle shark	filter feeder
Blue shark	fastest shark
Daggernose shark	largest extinct shark
Hammerhead shark	smallest shark

Answers: whale shark—filter feeder; Megalodon— largest extinct shark; pygmy shark—smallest shark; shortfin mako shark—fastest shark; great white shark—largest teeth; porbeagle shark—fast chaser of shoal fish; blue shark—migrates the greatest distance; daggernose shark—lives near Venezuela; hammerhead shark—wing-shaped head

Glossary

abdominal cavity
(ab-DAH-mu-nul KA-vih-tee)
The body part that holds the
stomach, liver, and intestines.

ampullae of Lorenzini
(am-PYOO-lee UV
lor-en-ZEE-nee) Jelly-filled
sacs connected to the snout of
a shark that can detect very
weak electrical fields, as weak
as half a billionth of a volt.

anal fin (AY-nul FIN)
A fin that grows under a
fish, near the tail.

buoyancy (BOY-unt-see)
An upward-acting force
caused by water pressure that
helps things stay afloat.

cartilage (KAHR-tuh-lij)
A type of body tissue that is
not as hard and rigid as bone,
but is more rigid and less
flexible than muscle.

caudal fin (KAW-dul FIN)
The tail fin of any fish that is
used for pushing it through
the water.

dorsal fin (DOR-sul-FIN) Fin
located on the back of a fish.

fossil (FO-sul) The preserved
remains of any living creature
that has been dug up.

gills (GILZ) A body part
found in all fish that extracts
dissolved oxygen from
water and releases carbon
dioxide. It is used by a shark
for breathing.

lamellae (luh-MEH-lee)
Fine layers of membranes
that improve a shark's ability
to smell.

lateral line
(LA-tuh-rul LYN) A fluid-filled
canal lined with tiny hairlike
receptors used as a sensing
organ to detect vibrations and
movement in the water. The
lateral line is located just
under the skin of sharks.

migration (my-GRAY-shun)
The regular movement around
the world of animal groups,
often in search of food or
desirable breeding grounds.

pectoral fins
(PEK-tuh-rul FINZ) Located on
either side of a fish's body,
the pectoral fins are like a
fish's arms. Some fish use
them for walking on, others
use them for flying, such as
the flying fish.

pelvic fins (PEL-vihk FINZ)
Located on the underside of a
fish, near its belly, these are
the equivalent to hind legs on
a four-legged animal.

plankton (PLANK-ten)
Tiny drifting animal and plant
organisms that are a source of
food for fish and some sharks.

POD (PEE-OH-DEE)
An acronym for Protective
Oceanic Device. This device
emits a small electric current
that is said to repel sharks.

rete mirabile
(REE-tea muh-RAH-bu-lee)
A network of fine blood
vessels found in many
different animals. It is used
by fish to regulate their
body temperature.

submersible
(sub-MER-sih-bul)
A commercial or non-military
device for traveling
underwater, sometimes to
great depths. They can be
manned or unmanned.

tapetum lucidum
(tuh-PEE-tum LOO-si-dum)
A layer of tissue in the eyes
of a shark that improves the
shark's ability to see in
low light.

Index

A
angel sharks 10, 20, 28
attacks 27

B
basking sharks 18, 28
black dogfish sharks 7
blacktip reef sharks 7, 22
blue sharks 18, 22
bramble sharks 10
broadnose sharks 10
bull sharks 22

C
cartilage 12
caudal fin 6, 12
chain catsharks 6
Cladoselache 8
cookiecutter sharks 22
Cretoxyrhina 9
crocodile sharks 22
Ctenacanthus 8

D
daggernose sharks 28
dorsal fin 6, 12

E
electroreceptors 15

F
false catsharks 7
filter feeder 7
frilled sharks 7

G
gills 7, 13, 21
goblin sharks 22
great white sharks 7, 17, 19, 29
gulper sharks 29

H
hammerhead sharks 11, 14, 19
Helicoprion 8
horn sharks 7
Hybodus 9

I
inner ear 14
intestines 12

J
jaws 12, 16

K
kitefin sharks 17

L
lamellae 14
lantern sharks 22
lateral line 15
liver 12,13

M
mako sharks 15, 21
Megalodon 9
megamouth sharks 18, 22
migration 22

N
Nostolepsis 8
Nothosaurus 9
nurse sharks 22

O
oceanic whitetip 6, 22
ornate wobbegong 11

P
pale goblin sharks 17
pectoral fin 17, 20

pelvic fin 6
porbeagle sharks 20
Port Jackson sharks 10
protective oceanic devices (POD) 24
Protospinax 9
pygmy sharks 22

R
rete mirabile 13

S
salmon sharks 12, 13
sandbar sharks 22
sand tiger sharks 28
sawsharks 11, 20
shark products 27
shortfin mako sharks 11, 15
spined pygmy sharks 7, 25
spiny dogfish sharks 22
spiral valve 13
Stethacanthus 8
stomach 12, 13
striped smooth-hound sharks 28
submersible 25
swimming 20, 21

T
tagging sharks 25
tapetum lucidum 15
taste 15
teeth 17
Thelodont 8
thresher sharks 6, 20
tiger sharks 17, 18, 19

W
whale sharks 6, 18, 19, 22

Z
zebra sharks 6

Websites

Due to the changing nature of Internet links, PowerKids Press has developed an online list of websites related to the subject of this book. This site is updated regularly. Please use this link to access the list:

www.powerkidslinks.com/disc/shark/